THE HERB BASKET

Basil

Bay & Borage

THE HERB BASKET

Basil

Bay & Borage

PHOTOGRAPHY BY GLORIA NICOL

Text by Hazel Evans

JG PRESS

The Herb Basket
Basil, Bay, and Borage

Designed and created by
The Bridgewater Book Company ltd.

Written by Hazel Evans
Photography by Gloria Nicol

Designer: Jane Lanaway
Project editors: Veronica Sperling/Christine McFadden
Page makeup: Chris Lanaway
Step illustrations: Vana Haggerty
Border illustration: Pauline Allen
Cover: Annie Moss
American adaptation: Josephine Bacon

CLB 4501
© 1996 Colour Library Books ltd
Published in the USA 1996 by JG Press
Distributed by World Publications, Inc.

The JG Press imprint is a trademark of
JG Press, Inc., 455 Somerset Avenue,
North Dighton, MA 02764

Color separation by Tien Wah Press
Printed and bound in Singapore by Tien Wah Press

ISBN 1-57215-108-0

CONTENTS

THE JOY OF HERBS	10
INTRODUCING BASIL	13
INTRODUCING BAY	16
INTRODUCING BORAGE	18
PLANT CARE	20
HARVESTING	22
PRESERVING	24
PLANNING A SMALL HERB GARDEN	26
AN HERB HANGING BASKET	28
GROWING A STANDARD BAY	30
SALADS	32
CHICKEN AND BASIL STIR-FRY	34
HERB AND VEGETABLE STIR-FRY	35
PESTO AND PASTA	36
THREE-NUT PESTO	37
MARINADES AND BOUQUET GARNI	39
BORAGE FRITTERS	40
RICE PUDDING WITH BAY	41
HERB CHEESES	42
BORAGE FLOWER SYRUP	44
OILS AND VINEGARS	46
AN ICE BOWL	49
A DECORATIVE DRIED BAY TREE	50
A CLASSIC BAY WREATH	52
DECORATIVE CANDLE RINGS	54
BORAGE AND BAY POTPOURRI	57
BORAGE FLOWER PIN CUSHION	58
INDEX	60

THE JOY OF HERBS

Basil

Bay

Borage

WELCOME TO THE wonderful world of herbs which have been important in our lives since ancient times. It sharpens your sense of history to know that the plants you are growing in your garden today flourished more than 2,000 years ago in Ancient Greece and Rome, and in the East where the Chinese used them as medicine as early as 3,000 BC.

Herbs have so much to offer. On the food front, they can spice up the simplest meal and turn it into a gourmet feast. But herbs are healers too, and many medicines today contain the same plant materials that has been used for centuries.

Herbs came to us in this country through the medicines of the native Americans and from Europe where, in medieval times, the monks grew them in walled gardens in order to make medicines to help the sick and the poor. They segregated the herbs in orderly beds so they could identify each kind with ease, a practise that developed into the decorative knot gardens of Elizabethan times. Inevitably, these precious plants found their way into the yards of ordinary people living nearby, and it was then that herbs began to have a wider use. The lady of the house first employed them as medication, but soon found they tasted and smelled good, kept insects at bay, and could be used in beauty potions and perfumes.

This book is about three of the most popular herbs: basil, borage, and bay. Their flavors are very different – basil is hot and peppery, borage has a delicate cucumber-like flavor, and bay is warm and provocatively pungent.

BASIL, BAY, AND BORAGE

A FAMOUS HERBALIST

One of England's most famous herbalists was Nicholas Culpeper, born in 1616. His Complete Herbal was full of remedies. From "blastings by lightning" to "the barking of mad dogs", Culpeper had a cure.

LEFT *Basil, borage, and bay all grow well in pots.*

Grow several kinds of basil in the same container.

BASIL, BAY, AND BORAGE

INTRODUCING BASIL

NE OF THE greatest of all the culinary herbs, basil is a plant of the sun. In France and Italy, you will find it on market stalls and on every housewife's windowsill as a first sign of spring. Adopted by the Mediterranean countries since the 1500s thanks to the spice traders from the East, the food of Provence, Italy, and Greece would be unthinkable without it today. It was not always used in cooking. In ancient times, Galen claimed it was "not fitting to be taken inwardly."

Basil is also traditional in India where it is called *tulasi*. The Hindus grow it in and around their sacred temples, and it is laid on the breasts of their dead as a protection against evil.

Every good Hindu goes to his rest
With a basil leaf on his breast
This is his passport to paradise

The name comes from the ancient Greek, *basilikon phuton* meaning "royal herb", and in Greece today bus-drivers keep a sprig of it on the dashboard for luck. It was known in ancient Rome too, and is believed to have sprung up around Christ's tomb when his body was laid there. The Romans thought that the perfume of its aromatic leaves evoked love, and that a man who took a sprig of basil from a woman was her love for life. It was also thought to bring sorrow, recalling perhaps the legend of Isabella immortalized by the poet Keats, who kept her lover's head in a pot of basil and watered it with her tears.

Basil has always had a powerful image. The herbalist Culpeper said that it "either makes enemies or gains lovers, but there is no in-between." Another herbalist, Parkinson believed it bred scorpions under its leaves.

In Elizabethan England, basil was used as a protection against witches, and an infusion was taken as a cure for headaches. Today, the dried powdered leaves are often prescribed as a snuff to clear the head.

Basil may be difficult to grow outdoors in colder parts of the country and at high altitudes. It loves the warmth and the sun, nor is it happy in damp conditions.

BASIL, BAY, AND BORAGE

SWEET BASIL
Ocimum basilicum

This is the traditional basil that is used in cooking. It has distinctive bright green leaves. It partners tomatoes perfectly and goes well with fresh garlic.

BUSH BASIL
Ocimum basilicum var. minimum

The most popular alternative to sweet basil, bush basil has much smaller, finer leaves and as its name suggests, a bushy appearance. Roll soft cheeses in its leaves.

LEMON BASIL
Ocimum basilicum citriodorum

Also known as Indonesian kemangue, this basil has a very attractive lemon fragrance. Use it in herb teas and sauces.

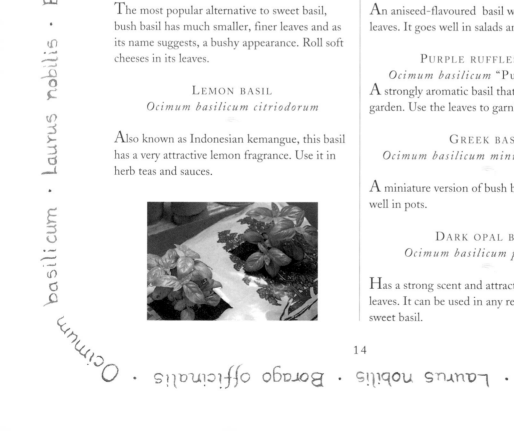

LETTUCE LEAVED BASIL
Ocimum basilicum neapolitan

This variety of basil, which comes from southern Italy, has larger floppier leaves than sweet basil and needs plenty of moisture and warmth. It makes a good pesto sauce.

GREEN RUFFLES BASIL
Ocimum basilicum 'Green ruffles'

An aniseed-flavoured basil with large ruffled leaves. It goes well in salads and stir-fries.

PURPLE RUFFLES BASIL
Ocimum basilicum "Purple ruffles"

A strongly aromatic basil that looks good in the garden. Use the leaves to garnish pasta.

GREEK BASIL
Ocimum basilicum minimum "Greek"

A miniature version of bush basil which grows well in pots.

DARK OPAL BASIL
Ocimum basilicum purpureum

Has a strong scent and attractive dark purple leaves. It can be used in any recipe calling for sweet basil.

SACRED BASIL
Ocimum sanctum

This can be found growing round Buddhist temples in Thailand and Hindu temples in India. It is a small, attractive plant with pinkish-purple flowers and deep purple stems.

ABOVE *Handle the basil carefully after washing to avoid bruising.*

HORAPHA BASIL

An anise-scented basil from Thailand, it can be cooked as a rather pungent vegetable or used in curries.

CINNAMON BASIL
Ocimum basilicum 'Cinnamon'

A cinnamon-scented basil from Mexico. Use it in any dishes where you might use the spice.

15

INTRODUCING BAY

GROWN IN WESTERN EUROPE since the 16th century, the aromatic bay is said to originate from Asia Minor. A handsome evergreen, it has dark waxy leaves, attractive small yellow flowers, and dark purple berries in the Fall. It takes well to clipping into shape. It seldom grows more than 26 feet tall and then only reaches that height in a sheltered spot. It grows particularly well in pots which make it a very decorative addition to a patio. Bay also comes in a golden version which is slightly less hardy.

The history of bay is inextricably linked to that of ancient Greece. It was dedicated to Apollo, and the oracles at Delphi, Apollo's temple, ate its leaves before giving out their prophecies. Bay has a mildly hallucinogenic property which may be the reason they did this. The roof of the temple, too, was covered in bayleaves because the herb was believed to keep witches and lightning away.

In Roman times the famous bay wreath was awarded to victors, not just in athletics but in the arts as well. The word laureate comes from bay's Latin name *laurus nobilis*, and it has always been a symbol of wisdom and glory.

Bayleaves were used before holly to decorate houses and churches at Christmastime because of their alleged protective properties – Culpeper says that "neither witch nor devil, thunder nor lightening, will hurt a man in the place where a bay-tree is." He also believed that the berries were effective against "venomous creatures and the stings of wasps and bees."

Bay has always been considered to be a strong antiseptic and was used to protect people against the Plague. An infusion of the leaves is said to aid the digestion. A massage with its oil is also said to relieve rheumatic pains, sprains, and bruises.

COOKING WITH HERBS

Always use fresh herbs if you can, to get the essential flavor. If you have to cook with dried leaves, halve the quantities of herb given in the recipe.

TIP
Add a bay-leaf to the water when poaching fish.

RIGHT *Fresh bayleaves can be bought from specialist stores.*

INTRODUCING BORAGE

THE WORD BORAGE is believed to come from the Celtic word "borrach" meaning bravery. There is an old English saying "I, borage, bring always courage." A draught of the herb is said to have an exhilarating effect and for this reason an infusion of borage was given to the Crusaders before they set off to war. In earlier times it was the basis of a drink called "nepenthe", a wine that was said to bring absolute forgetfulness and which was given by the Queen of Egypt to Helen of Troy.

Borage is at home mainly in Mediterranean countries where it grows wild and is known as bee-bread because it is much loved by bees. It is also called star flower, because of the shape of its brilliant blue flowers tinged with pink which are said to be the color of the Virgin Mary's robes. These distinctive small flowers have been featured throughout the centuries in needlework, and if you look carefully you will find them in many medieval tapestries.

Borage has always signified contentment. The ancient Roman writer Pliny claimed that it made one "happy and glad." Coles, the 17th century herbalist said that it was "very cordiall and helpes to expell sadness and melancholy," for it was believed to revive and cheer hypochondriacs.

A poultice of borage leaves was used in medieval times to soothe swellings and sprains. In France today, an infusion is often taken for fevers and chest complaints. But its main claim to fame must be in classic cool drinks. In Shakespeare's time it was added to tankards of cider, today you will find it decorating the wine cup that signifies summer in England: Pimm's.

18

BASIL, BAY, AND BORAGE

PIMM'S NO.1

Makes 1
ice cubes
1 measure Pimm's
3 measures clear lemonade
slice of lemon
sprig of borage

Put three or four ice cubes in a tall glass, pour the Pimm's over them, then the lemonade, and stir. Add a slice of lemon, and decorate with freshly cut borage.

FAR LEFT *Borage flowers are a beautiful blue tinged with pink.*

LEFT *Borage is difficult to buy, so it's worth growing your own.*

19

BASIL, BAY, AND BORAGE

PLANT CARE

BASIL
Ocimum basilicum

ABOVE *Basil can be grown easily from seed.*

Basil is a half-hardy annual. It grows up to 3 feet high, though dwarf varieties reach only half that size. It needs a sunny site but should be protected from the wind and from direct overhead sunshine that might scorch its leaves, so place it near a hedge or a wall. It prefers a light, well-drained soil, and hates heavy clay.

Basil cannot be put out into the garden until all danger of frost is past, and it has to be sown afresh each year. The seeds are slow to germinate – the Greeks and Romans thought you should curse them as you sow them to make them sprout faster.

Start the plant off from seed by sowing it under cover in early Spring, in a temperature of 55–60 degrees, using small pots or latticed "plug" trays. Avoid sowing it in open seed-boxes as the roots hate being disturbed.

Harden off the plants by moving them to a cooler place for a day or so, before placing outdoors. Alternatively you can sow them directly outdoors in late Spring.

As the plant grows, pinch out the tops of flowering spikes to encourage them to bush out. Watch out for slugs and snails on young plants.

Water basil in the heat of the day, it should no longer be wet by the time the sun goes down.

Cut plants hard back in the Fall and bring them indoors to prolong their season.

20

BAY
Laurus nobilis

This evergreen tree can grow up to 26 feet high. It is hardy in the South and Southwest, but you can lose a young tree in a hard winter. Bay likes plenty of sun, but prefers protection from the wind. It appreciates a rich, moist but well-drained soil.

Propagating bay is a long, slow process. Start it from seed by scattering the seed on the surface of barely moist soil in pots. Upend a clear plastic sandwich bag over each pot and secure with an rubber band to act as a mini-hothouse. It needs to be kept at 65 degrees. Germination is slow and inclined to be unreliable. Remove the covering once the shoots are 1 inch high.

Bay is raised professionally from cuttings in greenhouses where it can be misted constantly for a humid atmosphere. Raising it in pots under a plastic tent gives it the best chance of survival.

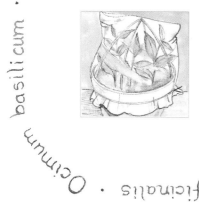

Grow bay from half-ripe cuttings taken in early Fall, covering the pot with a plastic bag. Keep warm until fresh shoots appear, then remove the bag. Plant out the following year.

BORAGE
Borago officinalis

Borage is a hardy annual, growing up to 3 feet high. It likes a sunny, open position in the garden. It is a large, hairy, somewhat ungainly plant with gray-green leaves whose lax growth and untidy appearance is compensated for by its flowers. There is a white-flowered version too (*borago officinalis* "Alba"), which is less often grown.

Grow borage in a light, well-drained soil that is not too rich. Choose a spacious patch because it will self-seed. Sow borage seeds 2 inches deep in the open where the plants are to grow in early Spring. Thin the seedlings to 24 inches apart.

Remove flowers as they fade to encourage a fresh crop, and to avoid having too many seedlings. Dig up and discard plants that have finished flowering, as they will blacken and look unsightly after the first frosts.

The cut stems of borage are quite rough, so handle with care. Put them on the compost heap in the Fall as they contain nitrogen.

HARVESTING

ENJOY YOUR herbs all year round. Harvest them when they are in their peak condition – usually in high Summer – and dry them to use in the winter months, or to make them into preserves. Generally speaking, it is best to pick any herb before it flowers, when the aromatic oils are at their best.

Cut fresh green basil leaves for the kitchen as soon as they unfurl. They wilt very quickly, so harvest them just before you plan to use them.

Cut leaves for drying just before the plant flowers and on a dry day once the dew has gone. Handle them as little as possible, since bruising them in any way will cause them to lose the essential volatile oil that gives them their flavor.

It is worth trying to get one last crop of basil at the end of Summer. In early Fall, cut the stems down to the base of the plant. Provided the weather is mild and there is some sun, you may get a crop of new shoots.

Allow some of your basil plants to flower so that you can collect seed for the following year. Once the seeds have fully formed, cut off the sprigs carefully and hang them to dry, fixing a paper bag over the tip of the stem, held in place with a small rubber band. That way the seeds will drop into it as they ripen. Sow in Spring.

ABOVE *Keep pots of basil on a convenient shelf ready for snipping.*

BASIL, BAY, AND BORAGE

TIP
Mist your bay
tree in hot, dry
weather and shield
the leaves from frost
during winter if
you want the tree
to thrive.

LEFT *Cut
borage should
be immersed
half way up the
stems in a pitcher
of water.*

Evergreen bayleaves can be harvested at any time of year. Take off individual leaves if possible, otherwise cut sprigs carefully so you do not damage the stem. Allow the leaves to dry before you use them as their flavor will then be stronger. If you have a large tree, sprigs of fresh bay make an ideal present if you are visiting with someone. Town-dwellers, in particular, are always glad to have a bouquet of fresh herbs.

Harvest borage as it comes into flower. Only use the youngest leaves for salads as the old ones will be prickly and tough. Save larger leaves instead for sprigs to put in summer drinks. Take both leaves and flowers off the plant as you intend to use them, for the blooms in particular tend to wilt. Pick the flowers when they are just fully opened in late morning when the dew has dried off them.

PRESERVING HERBS

BASIL TAKES a long time to dry – rushing things will turn the leaves black. Cut, rather than strip, the leaves from the stem. Or leave them on the stems for the time being. If they have to be washed use tepid water. Spread the leaves to dry on cheesecloth over a wooden frame, making sure that they do not touch each other. Keep them away from light during the drying period at a temperature that does not rise above blood heat – by a heat source such as a radiator or furnace in the Winter and on a shaded porch , or in a parked car left in a shady spot, on a dry Summer's day. Once dried, the leaves should be packed in airtight containers.

Basil will freeze well. The easiest way is to paint both sides of the leaves with olive oil then put them in plastic sandwich bags, making sure that they do not touch, and excluding as much air as possible. Dry them flat in the freezer. Once frozen, they can be packed in layers. Be sure to keep dried basil in jars that are well away from the light, the leaves fade quickly in the sunshine and look pallid and unpalateable.

TIP
Cut your herbs from the garden a few at a time, and prepare them straight away. Wilted stems will not preserve well if you are planning to freeze them afterward.

LEFT *Prepare herbs quickly and carefully for the freezer.*

BASIL, BAY, AND BORAGE

RIGHT *Borage flowers freeze easily in cubes to add to summer drinks.*

TIP
Borage is not the only herb worth freezing in cubes. Finely chopped basil, mint, tarragon and thyme can all be frozen this way to be used in sauces or marinades later on.

Pick bayleaves off the tree and lay them out on trays in a warm, shady place. Avoid excessive heat and direct sun or they will lose their oils and fade. Dry them at a relatively low temperature and they will keep their attractive dark-green color.

When bayleaves are dried they tend to curl, so press them lightly between two boards for two weeks before packing them into airtight containers.

Bayleaves can also be dried in bundles for immediate use or made into a wreath which you "raid" from time to time. The best quality leaves will be those stored in jars. Bayleaves make welcome gifts for dedicated cooks, so look out for attractive jars to put them in.

Borage leaves are difficult to dry as the plant is so succulent. They tend to turn black and lose their aroma if dried at too high a temperature. Dry them in at low temperature in a well-ventilated room, on cake racks or wire mesh. Then crumble into airtight jars and store away from the light.

Preserve borage flowers in ice-cube trays. Place them facing upright in the sections, cover with water and freeze. Then tip the cubes out into plastic bags for the freezer. Drop them individually into cold drinks.

BASIL, BAY, AND BORAGE

A VERY SMALL HERB GARDEN

Borage

Sage

Mint

Lemon
scented
thyme

Common thyme

Basil

Margoram

Lemon balm

Mint

Bay tree

Chives

Common thyme

Basil

THIS VERY SMALL herb garden measures only 6 feet square but manages to encompass in it all the herbs you need to enliven up your cooking. Its focal point is a baytree in a pot but it could equally well be a small fountain or a sundial.

Use flagstones between the beds for an old-fashioned look, but if you are uncertain of your skill in cutting them to form a circle, substitute gravel instead, as it is much easier to lay.

If part of your garden is in shade, plant mint, chives, borage, and lemon balm on that side. They need plenty of water but will produce lots of good greenery for cutting.

HERBS MAKE perfect companions for a patio. There are many decorative ways of growing basil and bay in pots, and even borage looks good when it takes center stage in large tubs, surrounded by other herbs.

Paint your pots in bright colors – Mexican pinks and oranges, turquoise, and white all look good against foliage. Use acrylic paints, they allow clay pots to breathe and won't wash off.

Buy the largest container you can find – it will not need watering so often. Always group small containers together for maximum effect, and paint them in a matching or complementary color scheme.

BASIL, BAY, AND BORAGE

FAMOUS GARDENS

Two herb gardens in England worth visiting are that of Vita Sackville West at Sissinghurst, Kent, and the tiny herb plot at the American Museum near Bath. Herb gardens in the U.S. include Ballingrath Gardens in Mobile, Alabama, and the Kensington Museum Garden in San Marino, California.

LEFT *Herbs take to pots without any problems.*

27

AN HERB HANGING BASKET

AN HERBAL HANGING BASKET located outside the kitchen door is a useful and ornamental way to have herbs to hand when you are cooking. Alternatively, if the kitchen is well lit, you could suspend a basket over the kitchen sink on a miniature pulley for easy access. Permanent residents for a basket of this kind could include chives, mint, thyme, marjoram, and sage.

A basketful of several different kinds of basil makes an attractive feature for a terrace in mid-Summer. Sow the seeds directly into the basket, or buy in small plants from a nursery. Choose a mixture of purple and green ruffles, edged by the shorter, bushy kind, with tall sweet basil in the center.

MATERIALS

bucket
wire hanging-basket
sphagnum moss
black plastic sheeting
potting mixture
basil seeds

1. Sit the wire basket in the top of a bucket to steady it.

2. Lay in a lining of sphagnum moss then, inside that, a sheet of black plastic in which you have made small holes at 5-inch intervals.

3. Fill it with soil or potting mixture. Moisten, then sprinkle with the basil seeds. When the seedlings appear, poke some through the sides.

4. Keep the basket indoors in good light until all fear of Winter frost is past.

Baskets filled with
basil are irresistible in Summer.

GROWING A STANDARD BAY

MOP-HEADED bay trees, grown as standards in pots can cost a great deal of money but are easy to raise if you have a little patience. Start off from a rooted cutting.

In the Fall cut or carefully tear off a straight woody shoot about 8 inches long with a heel on it (ie a piece of stem). Strip off the lower sets of leaves that might be covered with soil when the cutting is inserted, then push one-third of the cutting into a 3-inch clay pot filled with a mixture of soil and sand and firm it down well. Carefully water it from the top and then firm it again.

Set your cutting in a shady place indoors – in a shed, a garage or on a cool shaded window sill. Cover the whole pot with a large plastic bag, using a piece of twig to keep the "tent" away from the leaves. In Spring, check the cutting by giving it a light tug. If it has rooted, take it out into full light.

Now transfer it into a 4-inch pot filled with potting compost to which you should add half a teaspoonful of superphosphate or slow-release fertilizer. Push a 24-inch bamboo stake down to the bottom of the pot alongside the stem, taking care not to touch the roots. Tie the bay cutting gently to it using raffia or knitting wool. Place the pot in a shaded place where it will have to reach for the light - this will make the stem grow longer faster.

At this stage take off any side branches down the stem, one by one at weekly intervals, but leave any leaves as they help feed the plant.

Once the "trunk" of your cutting has reached the height you want it to be, pinch off the top growing tip. Now start taking off the lower leaves leaving enough to bush out at the top.

As the side shoots grow, pinch out their growing tips to give you a bushy ball shape. Move the plant to a larger pot each time the roots outgrow their container - a warning sign is if the plant has a top-heavy look or has roots coming through the bottom.

TIP
Be sure to feed your topiary tree well, especially during its growing years. If you are starting with a bought-in plant, choose one that has one good straight stem, then transfer to a prepared pot and continue as above.

LEFT *A full-grown topiary tree will last a lifetime.*

1. Place your cutting on a cool shady windowsill. Cover completely with a plastic tent supported with a twig to prevent it touching the leaves.

2. Re-pot in potting mixture with slow-release fertilizer. Stake and tie with twine or wool.

3. Pinch off the growing tip when the cutting has reached the required height. Remove the lower leaves to encourage the top to bush out.

4. Continue to pinch off the growing tips to achieve a ball-shaped topiary tree.

TIP

While your bay is being trained, be sure to feed it regularly.

31

SALADS

THE PUNGENT FLAVOR of basil goes wonderfully well with entrée salads made with rice or pasta, and makes a perfect partner for tomatoes too. It also combines well with garlic - put the two together in a salad dressing for extra flavor. Use a crushed bayleaf this way to spice up a classic vinaigrette.

Try rubbing a salad bowl with a handful of freshly bruised basil leaves before you put your salad in it. Pick flowering basil tops to snip over Italian salad leaves like radicchio, and sprinkle them over a tomato-and-onion salad.

The delicate cucumber-like flavor of borage is best on its own in a cool green salad. Mix it with iceberg or Boston lettuce, for instance. Choose young fresh leaves, cut them up, and toss them into leaf salads which could include spinach, cabbage, lettuce, and watercress. The flowers can also be sprinkled over green salad, for decoration.

TIP
Save wilted, leftover salad and braise it gently in a heavy-based saucepan, then add chicken broth tomake it into a delicious summer soup.

CHICKEN AND BASIL STIR-FRY

DEEP-FRIED, shredded basil makes a delicious topping for quick stir-fried dishes. Cooked this way, it keeps its dark-green color and unique flavor. You could use a mixture of mushrooms, store-bought and wild, for this dish, or all button mushrooms.

INGREDIENTS

Serves 4

4 skinned chicken breasts

1½ tbs cornstarch

1½ tbs soy sauce

6 tbs Basil Oil (see page 46)

2 sprigs fresh basil

2 large onions, minced

2 cloves garlic, crushed

1 tbs grated ginger root

2 cups broccoli flowerets

6 cups chopped mushrooms

⅔ cup sherry

3 green onions (scallions), chopped

TIP

**Speed is of the essence when making
a good stir-fry. Prepare the ingredients
well ahead of time but cook them at the last
minute and serve them right away.**

✦ Cut the chicken into small strips. Stir the cornstarch into the soy sauce, then pour the liquid over the chicken pieces. Leave for 1 hour.

✦ Heat 4 tablespoons of the basil oil in a wok. Mince the basil and deep-fry it quickly. Remove with a slotted spoon and leave to drain on a paper towel. Drain the chicken, reserving the marinade, and stir-fry in the oil for 2 minutes. Remove and set aside.

✦ Add the remaining basil oil to the wok and heat it.

✦ Add the minced onions to the wok with the garlic and ginger. Cook for 2 minutes.

✦ Add the broccoli and mushrooms, together with the remaining marinade. Cook for a further minute.

✦ Season, and return the chicken pieces to the wok. Add the sherry. Stir in the green onions and cook for 1 minute with the lid on.

✦ Serve topped with the crisply fried basil leaves.

BASIL, BAY, AND BORAGE

HERB AND VEGETABLE STIR-FRY

INGREDIENTS

Serves 4

2 leeks
½ cups broccoli
1½ cups carrots
2 cups white cabbage
4 green onions (scallions)
6 tbs oil
1 tbs grated ginger root
2 cloves garlic, crushed
2 tbs chopped borage tips
1 tbs soy sauce
6tbs sherry

❖ Clean and thinly slice the leeks, then chop into small pieces. Slice the broccoli, cut the carrots into matchsticks, shred the white cabbage, and chop the green onions.

❖ Heat the oil in a wok, add the ginger and garlic, and cook for half a minute. Stir in the broccoli and carrot, and cook for 1 minute. Add the cabbage, borage, and leeks and cook for a further minute. Stir the soy sauce into the sherry and pour over the vegetables. Add the green onions and cook for 2 minutes. Serve immediately.

❖ Crisply fried shreds of basil (see left) could also be used as a garnish for this dish.

BASIL, BAY, AND BORAGE

PESTO AND PASTA

BASIL IS THE main ingredient of that classic Italian dish, pasta with pesto sauce. Although pesto sauce is best when freshly made, you can freeze it successfully. Try it in other ways too, such as spooned over split baked potatoes, as a pasta salad topping, even on French bread. If you make your own pasta, try using chopped borage leaves as a stuffing for ravioli – a delicious idea from southern Italy. Toss fresh basil leaves into pasta shells too, to add last-minute flavor and color.

CLASSIC PESTO SAUCE

INGREDIENTS

Serves 4

2 cloves garlic

¹/₂ cup fresh basil leaves

4 tbs pine nuts (pignolas)

¹/₂ cup olive oil

¹/₂ tsp salt

1¹/₄ cups grated Parmesan cheese

❖ Peel the garlic, and tear the basil leaves. Purée all the ingredients, except the cheese, in a blender, or crush them with a pestle and mortar, adding the oil gradually. Stir in the cheese, then spoon the sauce over hot pasta.

THREE NUT PESTO

THIS DELICIOUS variation on the basic pesto sauce comes from Liguria, a mountainous region of northern Italy famous for its olives and vines. It is also an area where nuts are used generously in cooking. Like the traditional pesto, this rich purée features basil and pine nuts, but has almonds and walnuts too, for additional flavor. Many other herbs can be used to make inventive versions of pesto, among them minced parsley, tarragon, and thyme.

INGREDIENTS

Serves 4

2 cloves garlic

½ cup fresh basil leaves

1 tbs pine nuts (pignolas)

12 blanched walnut halves

12 blanched almonds

½ cup olive oil

½ tsp salt

¼ cup softened butter

1¼ cups grated Parmesan cheese

❖ Peel the garlic, tear the basil leaves and purée all the ingredients as shown opposite, stirring in the cheese at the end.

❖ This sauce also makes a great filling for bell peppers or beefsteak tomatoes.

MARINADES

THE PUNGENT FLAVOR of bay makes it marvellous in marinades for meat dishes such as beef and pork, but it also goes unexpectedly well with fish. Bay also blends with strong spices such as chili and coriander (cilantro) , giving added zip to their flavors. Thread bayleaves between slices of onion, beef, and tomato on kebob skewers to cook outdoors. Spear sea-fish such as red snapper with bay sprigs, or simply lay the sprigs on a barbecue and arrange pork or beef steaks on top.

CLASSIC MARINADE FOR BEEF

❖ To each bayleaf add a sprig of herb – any of the classics, such as thyme or marjoram, go well with bay – plus 1 cup dry red wine, $\frac{1}{2}$ cup water and 2 tbs olive oil.

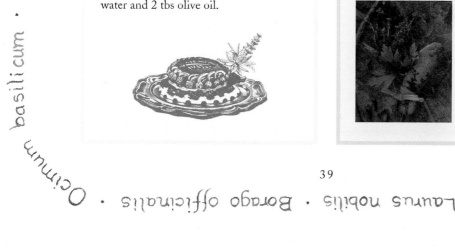

BOUQUET GARNI

THE TRADITIONAL bouquet garni is made from 2 sprigs of parsley, 1 sprig of thyme and a bayleaf, but try these variations:

FOR BEEF PROVENÇAL
Bay with parsley, thyme, 2 cloves, and 2 teaspoons of grated orange rind.

FOR LEMON PORK:
Bay, parsley, thyme, and a strip of lemon rind.

TO MAKE A BOUQUET GARNI

❖ To make your bouquet garni, wrap the herb sprigs in a piece of leek leaf to make a small package or tie together with

string or wool. If you include small items like garlic or cloves, place the ingredients in a square of cheesecloth, and tie with wool or string.

BORAGE FRITTERS

THE DELICATE cucumber-like flavor of young borage leaves comes out perfectly in these light-as-a-feather fritters. You can also substitute borage flowers for the leaves in this delicious dessert. Serve your fritters sprinkled with sugar, and with sour cream on the side, or with a slightly sharp fresh fruit salad.

TIP
Prepare the borage leaves just before frying otherwise they will go soggy.

INGREDIENTS

Serves 4
handful of young borage leaves or flowers
2 egg whites
about 2 cups frying oil
about 2 cups all-purpose flour
about 1 cup confectioner's sugar

✧ Rinse the borage leaves well beforehand, blot them on a paper towel, and leave to dry.
✧ Whisk the egg whites until they stand up in stiff peaks. Have a heavy skillet or a deep fat fryer at the ready.
✧ Heat the oil until a piece of bread dropped into it, turns golden-brown in 60 seconds. Working quickly, dip the borage leaves in the flour, shake them, then dip them in the beaten egg white. Deep-fry them, keeping them separated as you do so.
✧ Lift the fritters out with a slotted spoon, drain on crumpled, absorbent paper, and serve at once, sprinkled with confectioner's sugar.

RICE PUDDING WITH BAY

USED INSTEAD of the traditional nutmeg, a bayleaf gives an attractive new flavor to a "down home" favorite. You can store short-grain rice in a jar with fresh bayleaves in it, to enhance the taste still further. Bayleaves can also be used to flavor home-made ice cream. Remove them from the mixture before you freeze it.

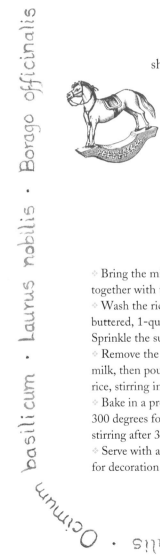

INGREDIENTS
Serves 4
5 cups full-cream milk
1 bayleaf
3 tbs short-grain rice
2 tbs superfine sugar
2 tbs butter

◈ Bring the milk to the boil in a saucepan together with the bayleaf, then allow to cool.
◈ Wash the rice and put into a buttered, 1-quart ovenproof dish. Sprinkle the sugar over it.
◈ Remove the bayleaf from the milk, then pour the milk over the rice, stirring in the butter.
◈ Bake in a preheated oven 300 degrees for about 2 hours, stirring after 30 minutes.
◈ Serve with a bayleaf on top for decoration.

TIP
For an extra-creamy rice pudding, replace some of the milk with evaporated milk.

HERB CHEESES

BASIL AND BORAGE can be used to make delicious herbed cheeses. Use stronger kinds of cream cheese or goat's cheese with basil. The lighter cottage or cream cheese complements the more delicate flavor of borage.

Wrapped around small farmer cheeses and stored for two or three days, basil will give them a more delicate delicate flavor. If you use the tiny-leaved bush basil, you don't need to chop the leaves, you can use them whole.

GOAT'S CHEESE WITH BASIL

THESE GOAT'S cheeses can be preserved in wide-necked jars then covered with basil oil (see page 46). Don't confine yourself to the conventional sweet basil to flavor cheeses, try the subtle flavors of anise basil or cinnamon basil instead. Purple-leaved basils look good too, wrapped round small cheeses for a decorative effect.

Pound the goat's cheese with a pestle and mortar, adding black pepper to taste. Form into small rounds and roll in the chopped basil.

INGREDIENTS

Makes 1 cup
1 cup fresh goat's cheese
2 tbs minced basil leaves
freshly-ground black pepper

TIP
Use herb-flavored goats' cheeses in cooking whenever you can. They make a delicious filling for an omelet, for instance, or a base for a soufflé. They are also good stirred into hot spaghetti.

42

COTTAGE CHEESE WITH BORAGE

BORAGE GIVES cottage cheese a subtle, cucumber flavor. Serve in small bowls or chill thoroughly and put into a mold. Store for at least a day before using, then serve decorated with borage flowers. You can serve it, too, spread on thick fresh cucumber slices to accentuate the flavor even more. Sit the cucumber slices on tiny rounds of toast to turn them into canapés.

INGREDIENTS

1 cup small-curd cottage cheese
4 tbs minced young borage leaves

Place the cottage cheese and the borage leaves into a blender and process until well mixed and smooth, or pound the cheese with the herb in a mortar with a pestle. Season to taste.

TIP

If you're not planning to make your cheese immediately, freeze the borage in plastic bags until you are ready to use it. You can mix it with the cheese before it has completely thawed.

BORAGE FLOWER SYRUP

ERARD THE HERBALIST wrote "A syrup made of the floures of borage comforteth the heart, purgeth melancholy and quieteth the lunaticke person." This syrup, which has a pretty pale blue tint, is delicious poured over ice cream or with fruit compote or salad. Decorate the dish with fresh borage flowers.

INGREDIENTS

1 cup fresh borage flowers
boiling water
sugar

1. Put the freshly picked borage flowers into a small bowl and cover them with boiling water. Leave them to soak for as long as possible, preferably overnight.

2. Next day, strain off the liquid, boil it, and pour it over more blooms. Finally, strain it, and press the flowers through a sieve to extract all the liquid.

⁕ Put one cupful of freshly picked borage flowers in a small bowl and cover with boiling water. Leave them overnight to steep.

⁕ The next day, strain the liquid off the flowers into a pan, and bring to the boil. Pour the boiling liquid over another cupful of borage blooms, then leave to soak for 8–10 hours.

⁕ Strain the liquid for the second time, pressing out all the juices from the flowers with the back of a wooden spoon.

⁕ Measure the liquid, and add 1 cup sugar for each 1¼ cups water. Heat slowly until the sugar has dissolved, then boil the syrup fast until it thickens. Remove from the heat, skim, cool, and store in bottles or jars.

HERB TEAS

Herb teas are a delicious alternative to conventional tea and many have a medicinal value too. –Basil and bay teas both aid the digestion.

⁕ Put a handful of herb leaves in a jug, pour 2½ cups boiling water over them, leave to infuse for a minute or so, then strain and serve.

OILS AND VINEGARS

T HE BEST herb vinegars are made with the aid of the sun: simply fill a bottle full of your chosen herb, pour vinegar over it, and leave the bottle on a sunny windowsill or porch for two weeks, turning it from time to time. Then bring it indoors, filter it, and re-bottle, adding a fresh sprig for decoration.

BAY VINEGAR

INGREDIENTS

Makes 2 $^{1}/_{2}$ cups
bay leaves
2$^{1}/_{2}$ cups vinegar

Put the herb in a bowl then heat the vinegar to boiling point. Remove from the heat and pour it over the leaves.
Leave them to steep until the mixture cools, then strain, and bottle with a fresh bay sprig inside.

BASIL OIL

INGREDIENTS

Makes 1 cup
large handful basil leaves
1 cup olive oil

Roughly chop the basil leaves. Crush in a mortar, gradually adding enough of the oil to turn them into a paste.
Spoon into a bottle and add the rest of the oil.

Stand the bottle on a sunny windowsill, turning and shaking it from time to time. Strain and check the flavor. If it is not strong enough, repeat the process using fresh basil. Finally, transfer the oil to a sterilized bottle and add a sprig of basil for decoration.

BASIL, BAY, AND BORAGE

HERB OILS

Basil leaves can be perfectly preserved in oil to use in cooking later on. Fill a wide-necked bottle with freshly picked sprigs and cover them with sunflower oil to preserve them. Remove them individually as you want to use them. Save the oil to use in a special salad dressing.

47

AN ICE BOWL

A COLORFUL HERB and flower ice bowl makes a marvellous centerpiece for a festive occasion and can be used to hold a variety of good things, from a Summer punch to a sorbet or a fruit salad. You could also make small individual versions for chilled soups and, of course, ice cream.

❖ Buy an ice bowl mold or take 2 bowls of the same shape, one of them 1 inch smaller than the other (flexible plastic bowls are easiest to handle).

❖ Half fill the large basin with iced water then float the small one inside it, weighing it down until the two rims are level. Secure it in place with adhesive tape.

❖ Now push borage flowers, basil and bayleaves into the water between the basins, using a knitting needle to help distribute them evenly. Add ice cubes to stop the herbs rising to the top.

❖ Place the bowls in a freezer, making sure that they are absolutely level.

❖ When you want to use your ice bowl, unmould it by wiping the inside of the small bowl with a wrung-out hot wet cloth, removing the coins as they loosen. Twist and take out the small bowl, then place the large one momentarily in warm water until it too can be twisted and detached. Place your ice bowl on a plate to catch any drips as it slowly starts to melt.

❖ If your ice bowl only makes a brief appearance, you can return it to the freezer to use over again.

TIP
You could substitute baby vegetables for flowers in the ice bowl using it to serve crudites – slivers of carrot, celery, radish, and root vegetables – served as an appetizer with an herb-flavored dip.

TO MAKE THE BOWL

Weight the smaller bowl so it is level with the larger one, and secure with tape.

A DECORATIVE DRIED BAYTREE

MAKE THIS little baytree to grace the dining table in the wintertime when flowers are expensive. You could dip bayberries in red acrylic paint then glue them on for a Christmassy effect. Or make it by pushing, rather than pinning, the leaves in place, and keep it in the kitchen, using the bayleaves for cooking as they dry.

MATERIALS

plastic sheeting for the pot
terracotta flower pot
plaster of Paris
suitably sized thick piece of stick (eg a stout twig)
cone or ball of Oasis (available from florists or craft suppliers)
sheet of carpet moss (available from florists)
stout twine
florist's wire, cut into 2-inch lengths
mature bayleaves
spaghnum moss

1. Line the flowerpot with plastic. Make up a stiff mix of plaster and pour it into the pot.

2. When the plaster begins to thicken, push in the stick and leave to dry. Push the Oasis on to the stick, making sure it overlaps by at least 1½ inches.

3. Wrap the carpet moss around the stick, then secure with the twine. Bend the florist's wire into U-shapes and use to pin the bayleaves in place, overlapping each row. Top the pot with spaghnum moss and decorate with a bow.

50

BASIL, BAY, AND BORAGE

TIP

Pick the bayleaves for the tree, and leave them for a few hours to get limp before you use them. They are more pliable and easier to work with that way.

51

A CLASSIC BAY WREATH

TRADITIONAL bay wreath makes a wonderful decoration at Christmas – the Romans used it at their mid-winter festival of Saturnalia. It also looks good in the dining room or kitchen at any time of year. Set off its good-looking green leaves with red ribbons, red berries, rosehips, or red chilis, or decorate it, as we have done, with dried citrus slices. (These will take about two weeks to stiffen in a warm place.) If you can't get a vine wreath base, substitute one made from cane or a wire base covered with spaghnum moss or ribbon. Or make a frame out of crushed chicken wire and fill it with moss. Cut off strong long leading shoots of a grape vine in the Fall, and wind them into wreath shapes while they are still fresh and green. Bind the ends with wire or ribbon. Store them until you need them.

MATERIALS

Makes 1
vine wreath base
2 bunches raffia, ribbon or twine
branches of bayleaves
12 dried citrus slices
thread
glue

1. Cover the vine base with raffia or ribbon, winding it around until it is well covered.

2. Pick shooting branches of bay leaves and cut them all to the same length – about 9 inches. Lash them to the frame by the base of the stem, using the raffia and making sure they all face in the same direction. Overlap them so that the base does not show. Tuck the last spray under the first one.

THE CHRISTMAS WREATH

The Christmas tree is thought to have originated in Germany, and came to the U.S. with German immigrants in the 19th century, The wreath's origins are far older.

BASIL, BAY, AND BORAGE

3. Thread several citrus slices together and tie. Dot glue at intervals around the wreath on center leaves and stick the citrus slices to it.

TIP

You will find the sprigs of bay easier to use if you pick them a day or two in advance, then let them dry off to enable them to stiffen before binding them to the base.

DECORATIVE CANDLE RINGS

ERBAL RINGS around candles not only look attractive
but serve a practical purpose, for they stop the
candlegrease from dripping onto the tablecloth.

TIP
To make
candle rings with
a decorative theme,
replace the borage
flowers with
small sprigs of
hollyberries.

MATERIALS
Makes 1
florist's wire
borage flowers
bayleaves
narrow ribbon
glue gun

❖ Thread young bayleaves onto florist's wire to
make attractive necklaces for the base of candles
to catch the drips of candlegrease.
❖ Bayleaves can be fanned out to form a mat on
which to stand a candlestick, or young leaves
could be threaded as above.
❖ Pressed borage flowers can also be used to
decorate candles. Glue them in place, then dip
the whole candle briefly into clear, fresh wax to
fix them in place.

*1. Measure the
circumference of the candle
and cut enough florist's
wire to loosely wind
around it twice. Make a
ring, tucking in the ends.*

*2. Bind the bayleaves
by their stems onto
the wire ring, using
florist's tape to secure
them to it.*

*3. Using a glue gun,
glue borage flowers
randomly over the
bayleaves.*

*4. Make a bow with
the ribbon and attach
it to the ring.*

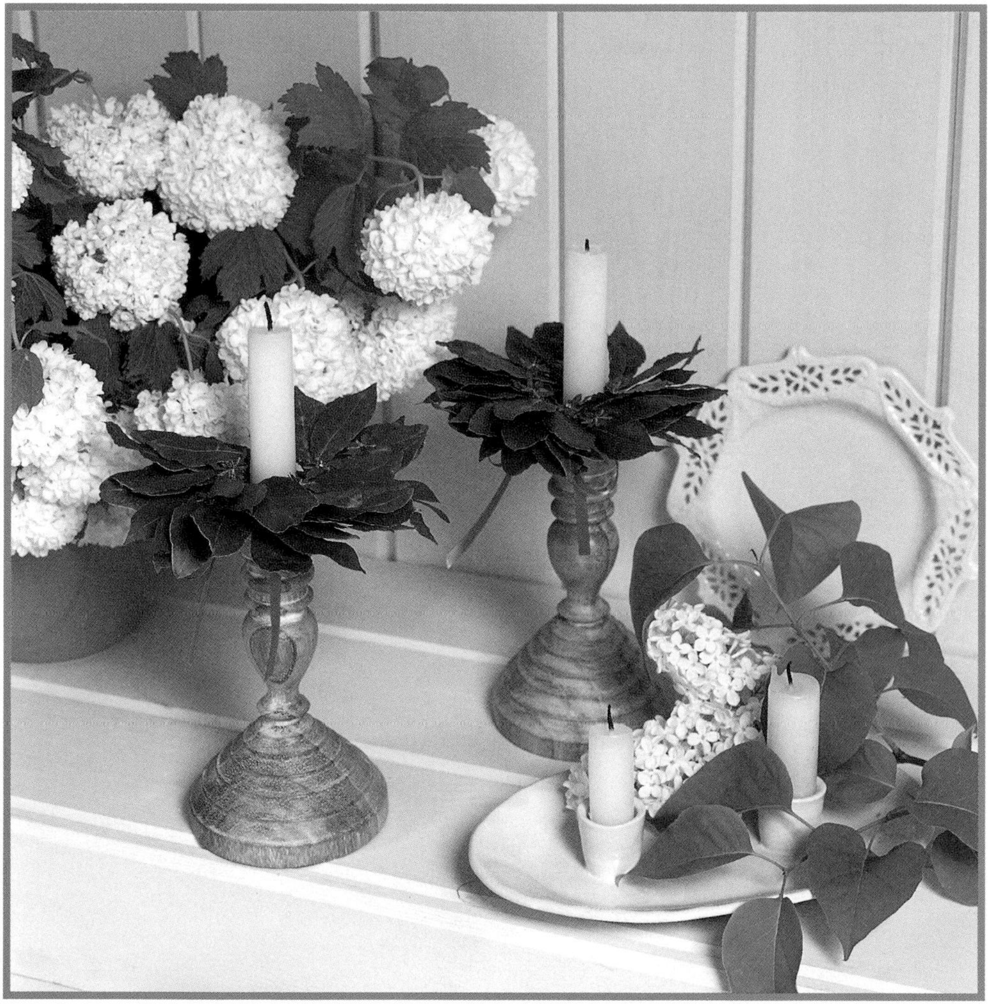

A POTPOURRI WITH BORAGE AND BAY

M AKE YOUR own potpourri to place around the house in decorative bowls, or in sachets for a lingerie drawer. In Winter, put some in a pot and keep it by an open fire, or in the linen-closet so that the warmth will release its delicious aroma.

T RY THIS UNUSUAL spicy potpourri. Put it into bags for a handkerchief or sock drawer. Leave it in baskets topped with borage flowers. Get into the habit of saving orange and lemon rinds, and leaving them on a sunny window sill to dry. They are a vital ingredient in many potpourris.

❖ Put the spices in a bowl with the orris root, add the essential oils, and combine thoroughly as though rubbing fat into flour.

❖ Mix together the dry ingredients then stir in the spice mix. Place the potpourri in an airtight container. Store it for 6 weeks, shaking it from time to time, then decant into baskets, and top with borage flowers.

INGREDIENTS

$\frac{1}{2}$ tsp grated nutmeg

$\frac{1}{2}$ tsp crushed cloves

2 tbs dried ground orris root

3 drops lavender oil

2 drops oil of bay

1 drop rose geranium oil

1 cup dried lavender flowers

1 cup dried crumbled bayleaves

1 cup dried lemon verbena, lemon balm, or lemon thyme

$\frac{1}{2}$ cup dried camomile flowers

$\frac{1}{2}$ cup dried borage flowers

1 tsp shredded dried orange rind

TIP
Dry some extra borage flowers in silica gel to maintain their color and shape, scatter them on the surface of the potpourri baskets.

BASIL, BAY, AND BORAGE

A BORAGE FLOWER PINCUSHION

SINCE MEDIEVAL times, borage flowers have been depicted in needlepoint and embroideries. Make this pretty pincushion using the flower design below. You could make this embroidery on a larger scale if you prefer, still using the same chart.

It can also be turned into a small herbal cushion by using canvas and wool instead of the linen and stranded cotton. Increase the size of the stuffing, backing material, and trimming accordingly.

MATERIALS
5-inch square of 32-count craft linen
square of backing material the same size
stranded thread in blue, black, green, and pink
small ball of stuffing
strip of edging material 24 inches by 1¼ inches wide
24 inches of fine piping braid

❖ Fold the linen diagonally in both directions to find the center and mark it lightly with a pencil.
❖ Now taking the center as your guide, stitch the flower design in cross-stitch (see right) using 2 strands of thread at a time.

❖ Cut the fabric strip into 4 pieces. Turn under ¼ inch and press along one edge of each. Butt it up to the decorative stitching frame round the design and stitch in place by hand, cutting and mitering the corners so that the strips make a "frame" for the embroidery.
❖ Right sides together, sew the embroidered linen to the backing material, leaving a gap for the stuffing. Trim, press, and turn right side out.
❖ Stuff the pincushion, sew up the gap, then slip-stitch the braid piping around the cushion to cover the seam.

BASIL, BAY, AND BORAGE

INDEX

B
basil 13–15
  goat's cheese 42
  hanging baskets 28
  harvesting 22
  ice bowls 49
  oil 46, 47
  pesto 36, 37
  plant care 20
  preserving 24
  salads 32
  stir-fry 34, 35
  teas 44
  tomatoes 37
bay 16–17
  bouquet garni 39
  candle rings 54
  dried trees 50–1
  harvesting 23
  ice bowls 49
  marinades 39
  plant care 21
  potpourri 57
  preserving 25
  rice pudding 41
  standards 30–1
  teas 44
  vinegar 46
  wreaths 16, 52–3
borage 18–19
  candle rings 54
  cheeses 42–3
  flower syrup 44
  fritters 40

harvesting 23
ice bowls 49
pincushions 58
plant care 21
potpourri 57
preserving 25
salads 32
stir-fry 35
bouquet garni 39
bush basil 14

C
candle rings 54
cheese 42–3
chicken stir-fry 34
Christmas wreath 52
cinnamon basil 15
cooking 17, 32–48
cottage cheese 43
Culpeper, Nicholas 11, 13, 16
cuttings 21

D
dark opal basil 14
dried bay trees 50–1
drinks, borage 18, 19

F
fish poaching 17
flowers
  pincushions 58
freezing herbs 24, 25, 43
fritters, borage 40

G
gardens 26–7
goat's cheese 42
Greek basil 14
green ruffles basil 14

H
hanging baskets 28
harvesting 22–3
headaches 13
herb cheeses 42–3
herb teas 44
horapha basil 15

I
ice bowls 49

L
lemon basil 14
lettuce leaved basil 14

M
marinades 39

N
nuts, pesto 37

O
oils 46–7

P
pasta 36
pesto 36, 37
Pimm's No. 1 19
pincushions 58
plant care 20–1
potpourri 57
pots 26
preserving 24–5
purple ruffles basil 14

R
rice pudding 41

S
sacred basil 15
salads 32
seeds 20–1
small gardens 26–7
standard bays 30–1
stir-fry 34, 35
sweet basil 14
syrup, borage 44

T
teas 44
three nut pesto 37
tomatoes, basil 37

V
vegetable stir-fry 35
vinegar 46

W
wreaths 16, 52–3

Ocimum basilicum · Laurus nobilis · Borago officinalis

BASIL, BAY, AND BORAGE

ACKNOWLEDGMENTS

The publishers would like to thank
the following companies for their help:

BASKETS AND GLASSWARE
Global Village,
Sparrow Works, Bower Hinton, Martock, Somerset, U.K.
Telephone: +44(1935) 823390

DRIED HERBS AND FLOWERS
The Hop Shop,
Castle Farm, Shoreham, Sevenoaks, Kent TN14 7UB.UK
Telephone: +44(1959) 523219

HERB PLANTS BY MAIL ORDER
Jekka's Herb Farm,
Rose Cottage, Shellards Lane, Alveston, Bristol BS12 2SY., UK
Telephone: +44(1454) 418878

HERB SEEDS
Suffolk Seeds,
Monks Farm, Pantlings Lane, Coggeshall Road,
Kelvedon, Essex CO5 9PG, UK.
Telephone: +44(1376) 572456